THE beach book

loads to do at lakes, rivers and the seaside

fiona danks and jo schofield

F

FRANCES LINCOLN LIMITED

PUBLISHERS

For Connie, Dan, Edward, Hannah and Jake

contents

Frances Lincoln Ltd
www.franceslincoln.com
www.goingwild.net

The Beach Book
Copyright © Frances Lincoln 2015
Text copyright © Fiona Danks and Jo Schofield 2015
Photographs copyright © Fiona Danks and Jo Schofield
2015

First Frances Lincoln edition 2015

A catalogue record for this book is available from the
British Library.

ISBN 978 0 7112 3577 9
Printed and bound in China

9 8 7 6 5 4 3 2

discovering beaches

Let's go on a beach adventure. What sort should we choose? You could explore rocks to discover hidden pools, dam a stream, make giant pictures in the sand or look for twisted driftwood monsters along the tideline. How about going out after dark to make shining sandcastles, or early in the morning to look for wild animals and birds? Or wrap up warm and go out in the middle of winter to make a shelter and a little fire on which to heat up some hot chocolate. Try visiting the seaside after a storm to see what treasures the waves have washed up on the shore. And of course, beaches are great places for pirates, smugglers, brave explorers and desert islanders!

Every beach offers endless opportunities for play, adventures and fun, whether you are at the seaside, next to rivers, beside lakes or even by mountain streams – anywhere, in fact, where water meets land. Beaches form when water and weather wear away rocks to make mud, pebbles, shingle or sand. We can use these materials and other natural beach treasures to play games, make sculptures and tell stories.

The Beach Book is packed with ideas for exploring and enjoying every kind of beach. We hope it will inspire new adventures and show why we need to look after these special places, with their wonderful wildlife and wide, open spaces, calling us to run free.

Beach adventure kit

Pack up an adventure kit so you are fully prepared to make the most of your day:

● Wear the right clothes; wrap up when the weather is cold, cover up in the heat and wear wet boots or jelly shoes to protect your feet.

● Take sunscreen, hats and lots of drinking water with you in summer.

● A shelter-making kit: perhaps a small pop-up tent, a tarpaulin, or a big plastic sheet for making a simple shelter to protect you from the sun, wind and rain, or even snow!

- A couple of heavy tennis balls.
- A bug box or a clear plastic container, plus an old sieve and a magnifying glass.
- A sturdy metal beach spade or a garden trowel.
- Scissors or penknife; string or thread; elastic bands, Scotch tape and a soft pencil.
- Fishing line.
- First aid kit.
- Marshmallows and other goodies to toast over a fire.

For all the projects in this book, follow the safety guidelines on pages 124-125, and always go to beaches with grown-ups. If going to the seaside, watch out for undercurrents in the water and make sure someone has checked the tide timetable; beaches are much more fun at low tide, but you need to know when the tide will turn.

Some activities are easy to try and others are more challenging; remember that what is easy for one person may be tricky for another. The activity code below provides some guidance as to levels of difficulty and risk, but always take care when playing at the beach and near water.

May be possible to do on your own.

Some tricky bits which might need a little adult help.

Adult supervision essential.

1

beach adventures

01

go exploring

Beaches are exciting places to explore. Scramble over craggy rocks, discover hidden pools and caves, or wade through streams and play in sand dunes.

● If you thought beaches were only at the seaside, then think again! If you don't live by the seaside, try exploring rivers or lakes, or scrambling up a tumbling mountain stream to discover hidden beaches along the shore.

● How about becoming fearless explorers setting out on imaginary adventures? Scramble over the rocks to discover unexplored territories, shark-infested lagoons and mystery pot-holes inhabited by 'hobbits'.

● Make a beach obstacle course from natural finds for you and your friends to tackle. At low tide, search among the rocks for hidden natural swimming pools.

● Try out some bouldering along an exposed rock face. Without going more than about 30cm/1ft above the ground, see how far you can scramble lengthways along the rock face without putting your foot down on the ground.

Safety tips Be aware of cliff edges, caves and tides. Avoid places that might get cut off at high tide. Make sure you are always with adults when exploring a beach.

damming and diverting streams

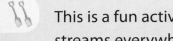

This is a fun activity for the whole family to enjoy in streams everywhere.

● The aim is to build a dam that stops or slows the stream, or diverts it so it takes a different route across the beach. Can you create a large shallow pool so it becomes a great place to paddle and play? How much water can you gather in the pool before the dam bursts? Trying working together, against the flow of the water, to make quick dam repairs.

● If you visit a beach at low tide where there are no streams, make your own by digging long shallow channels to collect the water that lies just below the surface of the wet sand, near the sea. Or how about digging out channels from the water's edge up to the beach, so they fill up as the tide comes in?

boat race competition

This is a great game to play in a group wherever there is a rushing stream.

● Collect natural materials such as driftwood, sticks and feathers. Look too for grasses or rushes to tie everything together. If you need to use string, you might find some on the beach, in the lunch rubbish, or in your adventure bag.

● Everyone can make their own little boat; try adding a keel and perhaps an outrigger to improve stability. Check that each boat floats, making adjustments if need be. Choose a course for the race, and mark the beginning and the end, perhaps with little flags (see page 117). Line up competitors across the stream and place the boats in the water; on the count of three, let go! Which boat will cross the finishing line first?

Safety tip Take great care when playing in streams.

cook over a fire

Sitting around a beach fire and listening to the sounds of the sea is a very special experience to share with friends and family. In summertime cook up a tasty meal as the sun goes down, or on a crisp winter's day, huddle around the warm glow and heat up some hot chocolate. Good investments are a fire bucket, a folding grill and a billy can or a Kelly kettle.

● **Safety First** NEVER make fire without grown-ups present. Always follow the fire safety guidelines on page 124.

● Only make fires on beaches where fires are permitted.

● There should be no trace of your fire after you leave the beach; the best way to make no impact is to make a small fire in a metal pan, a metal bucket or even an old hubcap.

● There may be driftwood on the beach; if not, you need to take fuel with you.

05

beach feasts

You may have had picnics at the beach, but how about trying some beach feasts with a difference? Check tide timetables and be flexible about timings; the tide is high approximately every 12.5 hours, so if the tide is in at lunchtime, you might be able to go to the beach for breakfast or supper instead! Here are a few ideas:

Dawn Be the first people on the beach and enjoy breakfast as the sun rises. By a river or a lake listen to the wonderful sounds of the dawn chorus.

Midnight feast Go out in the evening as the tide is going out

and enjoy a night feast round a small fire, and some of the night activities from this book. (See pages 100-111).

Midsummer celebration Go to the beach on the longest day with a special summer feast and make the most of all that daylight!

Foraging feast Catch some fish or gather shellfish to cook over a fire (see page 18).

Birthday parties and other celebrations No matter what the weather, you can always wrap up warm by a fire or play Beach Book games, such as treasure trails (see page 42) or funny feet (see page 98).

Whenever making a fire, follow the fire safety guidelines on page 124.

foraging

Here are a few ideas for gathering wild seaside food. For other ideas, see our book *Go Wild* or look out for foraging courses.

Marsh samphire This fleshy plant grows in salt marshes and mud flats. Harvest with a sharp knife in the summer at low tide; don't pull it up by the roots. Wash thoroughly and steam or boil for 8-10 minutes; it tastes a bit like asparagus and is delicious with fish.

Shellfish The best places to gather shellfish are clean unpolluted rocky beaches in the countryside, and when the tide is at its lowest.

● Only gather mussels longer than 3cm/1.5in in length; wash thoroughly in at least two changes of fresh water. Cook on a grill over an open fire or boil in a little water. Discard all mussels that don't open up on cooking.

● Carefully cut large limpets from rocks. Cook them in their shells on a grill over the fire or directly in the hot coals. Once cooked, use a knife to remove the soft guts on top and eat the muscled foot below. Rubbery but tasty, yum, yum!

Safety tips

● Get a good field guide to help with identification.

● Avoid polluted waters and only forage at low tide.

● When harvesting shellfish, choose the larger shells, giving the smaller ones a chance to grow.

● Never eat shellfish raw; cook thoroughly immediately after harvesting, and discard dead ones.

07

crabbing and fishing

Catching these wild creatures calls for quiet and patience, and tempting them with tasty looking bait. Take a fishing line and a small penknife to the beach. For more ideas see our book *Go Wild*.

Crabbing Place the soft body of a shellfish in a little net bag (perhaps a fruit net from your picnic) on some string. Lower the bag into the water to tempt out hungry crabs. Place them gently in a bucket of sea water to look at them before releasing them.

Fishing Try fishing off a pier or the rocks with a fishing line and some shellfish bait; take care when baiting the hook and when removing your catch from the hook.

Crayfishing The introduced signal crayfish, with its distinctive red claws (see page 9), spreads disease to native species and digs out riverbanks. To catch them, put a bit of bacon in a plastic tray on some string. Lower the tray into the river and pull it up when a crayfish arrives. Boil them in water for a few minutes for a tasty snack.

Safety tips Don't try fishing without a grown-up to help. Handle fishing hooks and crabs and crayfish with great care.

2

beach wildlife

beach bioblitz

What wildlife can you spot on and around the beach? This challenge involves finding as many plants and animals as possible over 24 hours; you could go along to an organized event or carry out your own bioblitz.

DIY beach bioblitz Make a big picture of the beach on the sand, showing details such as rocks, sand dunes, and the sea. Draw pictures of the wildlife you spot in different parts of the beach, including birds flying over the sea, fish in the water (and perhaps a galloping unicorn!). For help with identification go to www.ispotnature.org.

Become a scientific recorder Perhaps you could help scientists looking for information about beach wildlife. For example, The Great Egg Case Hunt needs information about shark's egg cases, often found washed up on the shore, see www.sharktrust.org.

You may also wish to add actual wildlife clues such as feathers, shells and seaweed to your bioblitz.

rock pooling

Discover the miniature wildlife worlds of trapped rock pools that are revealed at every low tide with these tips:

● The most interesting rock pools are on quiet, rocky beaches at the lowest tide. Creep up quietly to a pool. Sit down and watch, without casting a shadow over the water. Look out for little fish, darting shrimps, scuttling crabs, starfish, sea anemones with waving tentacles and hermit crabs hiding in shells.

● To take a closer look, push seaweed aside with a stick or catch some creatures gently in a net. Tempt animals out of their hiding places by placing a crushed limpet in the pool. Look underneath loose stones to find little crabs and other creatures.

● Look at the creatures in a clear plastic container of sea water before returning them to the pool.

Safety tips for you and the rock pools

● Watch out for tides and for sharp and slippery rocks.
● Always leave rock pools and stones as you found them.

make rock-pooling equipment

There's no need to buy fancy equipment; try making your own from bits and pieces.

Rock pool viewer This viewer cuts out the sun's glare or ripples made by the wind so you can spy on rock pool worlds. You will need a dark coloured plastic bottle, or a clear one decorated with acrylic paint. Cut off the bottom of the bottle to make a tube, covering the sharp edge with insulation tape. Stretch cling film over the bottom of the tube, fixing it in place with an elastic band to make a smooth viewing surface. Place the viewer's base just under the water's surface, and spy on the underwater world.

Rock pooling net and bucket Make a simple net from a fruit net from your picnic. Open one end of the net and weave a bendy stick through the holes around the edge. Tie on to the stick in several places to make secure. Attach the end of the loop onto the rest of the stick as shown. If you can't find a bendy stick, weave the net onto a forked stick. For a perfect bucket, use a cut-off plastic bottle to store your catch.

Safety tips Be careful when exploring rock pools. Don't lean too far over the water when using a rock pool viewer.

11

beachcombing hunt

The twice-daily tides drop all sorts of bits and pieces from near and far onto seaside beaches. The best time to beachcomb is at low tide after a winter storm.

Going Wild Scavenger Hunt
What can you spot?

- ☐ **Different shells.**
- ☐ **Sea potato shells** A type of sea urchin which looks a bit like a potato.
- ☐ **Seaweed** How many different types can you spot?
- ☐ **Mermaid's purse** The hard egg capsules of skates, dogfish, rays and some sharks.
- ☐ **Sea wash ball** Spongy egg masses of the common whelk.
- ☐ **Sponge** A soft natural sponge or sea weathered dead coral.
- ☐ **Sea life skeletons,** crab or lobster skeletons.
- ☐ **Driftwood** Look for sea-battered driftwood in interesting shapes.
- ☐ **Non-living materials** Sea-smoothed glass, interesting stones – perhaps perfectly round, perfectly white or a stone with a hole.
- ☐ **Minibeasts** Can you spot minibeasts sheltering and feeding among the seaweed and other tideline materials, and birds. coming down to feed?

Can you find a round sea urchin shell, conical limpet, long razor shell, a sunny scallop shell, or a knobbly oyster shell? Or how about the smallest shell you can find, a shell skeleton, or multi-coloured Mother of Pearl, found inside some mollusc shells. What is the most unusual thing you can find? Let us know at www. goingwild.net.

Safety tip There may be rubbish along the tideline; avoid anything dirty or sharp.

12 exploring sand dunes

Some beaches are backed by dunes, where wind-blown sand gathers in mounds and tough marram grasses trap and stabilize the sand.

Creep quietly through the dunes, looking out for lizards, birds, butterflies and all sorts of wildflowers and tough plants adapted to growing in these harsh, dry places. Have fun exploring the ever-changing dunes with their hidden valleys and ranges of small hills, perfect for playing tracking games and hide and seek. On a windy day, can you spot mini-sand dunes on the beach? Sand can be trapped around little things such as pebbles, seaweed or even a single feather.

Safety tips for people and sand dunes Sand dunes are precious landscape features and wildlife habitats; look after them and remember that they can be easily worn away and damaged.

river beach wildlife

Meandering rivers, babbling brooks and rushing streams provide homes for all sorts of wildlife on their beaches, banks, and beneath their water. Any creatures wanting to avoid being swept downstream must cling on tightly, swim fast or find a place to hide from the flow. Look out for:

Minibeasts such as freshwater shrimps, mayfly and dragonfly nymphs and caddis fly larvae. Look under rocks on the beach and at the water's edge, putting the rocks back as you found them. Try dipping a net or sieve in the water to see what you can find. Look for clues left behind by birds and mammals, such as footprints, or signs of feeding. Also look out for watery birds such as ducks, swans, kingfishers and dippers.

Safety Tip This activity should always be supervised by an adult.

3

beach games

ball games

How about making your own games equipment or inventing new ball games? Here are a couple of ideas:

Knee volleyball A great game for mixed age groups; everyone is on their knees so they are all equally disadvantaged! Draw a rough court on the sand with a spade or a stick, adding a small mound of sand across the middle to represent a net. Follow the same rules as normal volleyball.

Rounders and baseball Fancy a game but you have no bat or ball? Don't worry, just look around the beach and see what you can find! A bit of driftwood makes a good bat, and perhaps you could make a ball from plastic bags wrapped tightly around a pebble, tied together with string.

Search the beach for items to make into bats, balls and nets. If you can make up any fun new games we would love to hear about them!

15

ball runs

A great game for a sandy beach; how far can you make your ball roll?

● You need a small heavy ball. Build a large mound of sand. Use your hands to make a run winding down and around the mound; it should be exactly the right width for the ball, very smooth and with walls to keep the ball on track.

● Can you make the ball roll all the way from the top of the mound to the bottom? Add a few extra challenges; can you make a tunnel so the ball rolls through the middle of the mound? Or how about making two ball runs winding around the mound, and then challenging your friends to some races?

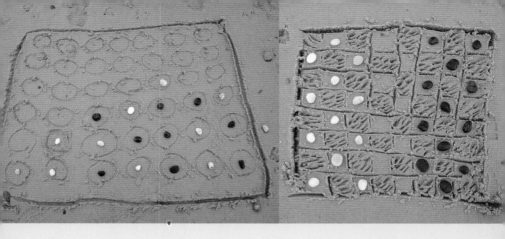

board games

If you think board games at the beach must be completely impossible, think again! A sandy beach provides a perfect board for pebble or shell counters. You could play noughts and crosses/tic-tac-toe, hopscotch, checkers, Connect Four, or even chess.

● Find a smooth area of firm, damp sand and draw a board using your finger or a stick. A board for checkers or chess is eight squares by eight squares. A Connect Four board has seven circles across and six circles going upwards.

● Hunt for natural playing pieces such as shells, pebbles, seaweed or even feathers. These black-and-white pebbles are perfect; for checkers you need 12 pieces for each player. Sort the pieces into groups according to type or colour. Now play your game!

17

made-up games

The challenge is to invent new games using whatever you find on the beach; here are a couple of ideas:

Beach barts A cross between boules and darts! Make a target by drawing concentric rings on a flat area of damp sand. Number each ring, with the highest number in the middle. Each person should find three stones, the rounder the better. Mark a spot to stand, about 2m/6ft from the outer ring. Take it in turns to throw your stones into the target. Who can get the highest score?

Hacky sock 'Hacky sack' is played with a small bag filled with rice, plastic pellets or sand. How about using a sock and playing Hacky Sock instead? Pour dry sand into the toe of a sock to make a ball about the size of a tennis ball. Twist the sock round

tightly and then turn it over on itself and twist again. Find some big feathers and push the quills into the loose end of the sock. Secure with string or an elastic band. Throw it around for a fun game at the beach.

Safety tip Always take great care when throwing stones.

beach skittles

How many versions of beach skittles can you invent?
Here are some ideas to get you started!

Rubbish skittles Pour a little dry sand into bottles,
juice cartons or plastic pots left from a picnic. How
many of these rubbish skittles can you knock
down with one ball?

Driftwood skittles Using charcoal from a fire we
drew funny characters on driftwood planks. We
stood them in a row and threw stones at them
to see who could knock down the most skittles.
Perhaps you could transform your driftwood
skittles into cartoons of your family or favourite
characters from books or films.

Stone skittles Make several stone towers in
a group; take it in turns to knock them down
by throwing stones at them.

Safety tip Always take great care when
throwing stones.

treasure trails

Treasure trails are perfect for beach parties but require a little forward planning.

Message in a bottle trail Lay a trail of arrows or flags (see page 117) leading to messages in bottles. Each message should contain a fun challenge to do, such as making giant feet (see page 98) or any other Beach Book activities.

Pirate maps Yo-ho-ho me hearties, can you discover the pirate treasure in this game for two crews of swashbuckling pirates?

● Each crew buries some treasure (a chest of golden chocolate coins perhaps?). Either mark the spot with a cross of stones, sticks or shells, or count the paces from a nearby feature.

● Each crew draws a pirate map on the sand, indicating where the treasure is buried. This map shows the sand dunes at the top of the beach, the beach huts, the sand with its pools of water, and the sea.

● Each crew use the other crew's map to find the treasure. Can you spot where the treasure is buried in this map?

20

stone towers

This is a great family project, but be careful to construct well-built structures that won't fall on you.

● Build towers in favourite or prominent places, perhaps on a rocky outcrop.

● Who can make the tallest tower? Use a large level rock as the base, and then collect flat stones of different sizes. Build slowly, taking time to choose exactly the right stones. Make each layer smaller than the one below, and place little pebbles around and under each flat stone to stabilize the structure.

● Build towers and cairns near the water's edge on a rising tide; which one will withstand the incoming waves for the longest time before toppling into the sea?

● Dismantle your towers before leaving the beach.

Safety tips This activity could be dangerous if not well planned; make sure adults are around. Check that each stone layer is secure before adding the next one.

21 skimming stones

This old favourite is best played across sheltered water in a bay, a lake or a river pool on a day with little or no wind.

● Collect some flat oval or spherical stones (see page 33); each one should fit easily in your hand. Hold a stone loosely between thumb and finger in the hand you usually use for throwing, tucking the other fingers under the stone. Throw from hip height, flicking your wrist and throwing the stone as horizontally as possible so that it jumps and skips across the water's surface.

● How far will your stone skim? Count the number of bounces; can you beat the 2007 world record of fifty one? Can you make your stones jump over a log or rock in the water? Have a competition with your friends, allowing each person five skims.

sundials and sun clocks

Experiment with stones and sticks to see how the shadows move during the day as the earth rotates.

Rough sundial When you arrive at the beach, draw a circle in the sand and push a stick or a long stone into its centre. Use pebbles, sticks or shells to represent the numbers around the face of the 'clock', noting the time when you make it. See how the shadow moves during your time at the beach.

Sun clock If you are going to the beach for the day, find a quiet spot in the open sunshine above the high tide mark. In the morning, push a straight 1m/3ft stick into the sand. Every hour on the hour, mark the tip of the stick's shadow with a short stick or a pebble, writing the number of the hour beside it if you wish. Return on a sunny day to see if the clock is accurate!

23

stone jenga

This beach version of the popular Jenga game uses small flat stones instead of wooden blocks. Take it in turns to add a stone to the top of the tower; if your stone makes the tower collapse you are the loser. To make the game more fun, each person can stabilize the previous player's stone by inserting smaller pebbles beneath it before adding their stone on top.

24 stone balancing

This fun challenge is easier than you might think! Choose a rock on which to balance your stone; look for a little imperfection, perhaps a nick or a groove. Choose a stone to balance; turn it in your hands to get the feel of it. Place it on the imperfection in the rock and move it around slowly. Take your time and try it as many

ways as you can; you will know when the stone is balanced. Now remove your hands and leave the stone standing there!

Safety tip Handle heavy stones very carefully.

funny faces

**The perfect game for pebbly beaches everywhere.
All you need is a pencil or some charcoal.**

Collect lots of pale-coloured pebbles. Draw hair, ears, eyes, noses and mouths of people and animals on separate pebbles. Keep drawing different features until you have a good variety of funny faces. Try swapping the features around to make crazy aliens and monsters. How beautiful the cat is with donkey's ears and a clown's mouth!

Funny Face game Turn all the pebbles over so you can't see the drawings. Take it in turns to pick a pebble; the first person to pick all the right features to make a funny face wins the game.

Memory game Take it in turns to choose a pebble; if it's not the right feature to match the face you are collecting, you have to turn it back over. The first person to get all the matching pieces to make a face is the winner.

4

beach art

pewter pendant casting

A fun activity suitable for sandy beaches where fires are permitted. You will need a small casting pot, heatproof gloves and long ingots of lead-free, jewellery-grade pewter, available from art suppliers (e.g. www.tiranti.co.uk).

Metal casting

- Make a small fire, preferably in a fire pan. Heat the pewter in the casting pot until it becomes molten; pewter's low melting point makes it ideal for casting.

- Push a natural shape, perhaps a shell, into slightly damp compacted sand to make a mold. Carefully pour the molten pewter into the mold. Hold a small stick upright in the mold as you pour to leave a hole for threading a string through.

- Don't move the pendant until it has gone cold and is set completely hard.

Safety tips Use heatproof gloves when handling the casting pot and doing the casting. This activity should be supervised by an adult. See the Fire Safety Guidelines on page 124.

beach pictures

Beaches beside rivers, lakes or the sea are often littered with natural materials that you may not have paid much attention to before. Look out for interesting bits and pieces to transform into beach pictures.

● Perhaps a clump of seaweed could become the jaws and tail of a sea crocodile creature? Or a twisted water-washed root might become legs for a giant spotted pebble beetle?

● Look at colours and textures; white pebbles or shells look amazing on dark wet sand, or try making a picture on a green grassy bank for contrast.

● If you can't find any natural materials that inspire you, how about using your own handprints or footprints to make pictures or write your name on a sandy beach?

beach treasure and jewellery

Look for special treasures along the tideline.

Seaside treasure Collect coloured stones and sea-moulded glass from the sea's edge. Display your treasures in a squashed plastic bottle of water and place against a window to let the light shine through.

Beach jewellery Mimi found a shell worn away by the sea to make a ring; look out for readymade beach treasure jewellery or make pendants and necklaces from small stones, sea-smoothed glass, shell skeletons or feathers.

● Take some cord or thread to the beach with you. Look out for special things to thread along the cord, or items that you could twist the cord around.

● Or take your precious collections home and ask an adult to help you fix pretty shells, stones or smoothed glass onto a cord with a good dab of very strong glue. Leave to set before hanging from a ribbon, cord or a chain.

29

beach mobiles and wind chimes

For a special memento of your favourite beach, make a mobile to hang in a window or a wind chime to blow outdoors in the breeze.

Beach mobile Collect a few favourite beach treasures; look for sea-smoothed driftwood and an assortment of shells, mermaid's purses, feathers and pebbles with holes in. Tie a length of string or wool onto each end of the driftwood so you can hang it up. Tie your beach treasures along the driftwood. Ask an adult to help make small holes in some of the shells with a bradawl if need be.

Wild wind chime Hunt for beach materials that make a noise. Tie them onto driftwood, making sure they strike each other when the wind blows.

Safety Tip take care if using a bradawl to make holes in shells.

30

driftwood monsters

Wild winter storms often hurl driftwood onto the shore. Smoothed and shaped by the waves, this moulded and twisted wood can look almost alive.

● Search the beach for driftwood. Let your imagination get carried away as you look at the twisted shapes; what creatures could you create?

● This old tree was transformed into a menacing monster that looked as though it had crawled from the sea to guard the beach. Tangled roots and seaweed became his hair, an old crab shell with some pebbles became his staring eye, and sharp stones his vicious teeth.

● Leave your wild sculptures behind for others to discover; imagine how surprised you would be to come across this flying sea serpent or bird dinosaur.

31

sand sketching

Look for a stick, a stone, or a spade to use as a pencil, and find a large, flat area of firm damp sand to use as your sketch pad.

Take inspiration from the beach, the sea or your own limitless imagination to draw whatever you wish, like this dog with very long ears.

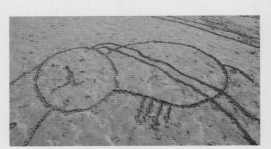

32 sand painting

Become a beach artist; with all that sand around, there's no need for paints and a canvas!

Collect some dry free-running sand in a container. If you look carefully you may find different coloured sands in different parts of the beach. Find a large flat area of smooth damp sand below the tide line to use as your canvas. Pick up some dry sand in your hands, or pour some into an old sock with a small hole, into a plastic bag or into a crisp packet with a corner cut off. Trickle the dry sand carefully over the canvas to 'paint' pictures.

sand silhouettes

Use dry pouring sand to 'paint' silhouettes around hands (see page 53), feet, toys or natural materials placed on the darker damp sand below the tide line. Or try making whole body silhouettes; ask a friend to lie down on damp sand and to shut their eyes tight while you pour dry sand all around them. Can they get out of the way without spoiling their silhouette?

rock art and poems

Find a large rock to use as a canvas or a flat stone to use as a drawing board or writing slate.

● Spread wet sand over a rock to make a canvas. Draw pictures in the sand with your finger, a pebble or a stick. Use a pebble to draw pictures or write a poem on a rock. Make sure to do it below the tideline so the waves can wash them away.

● Connie wrote a limerick on a stone writing tablet. If you can do better than this please send it in to www.goingwild.net.

Connie's poem

A lonely young crab was in strife
Too ugly to find a new wife
He found a bright shell
Squeezed his bum in quite well
Now hermit has a girl in his life...

67

35

sand sculptures

As all sandcastle builders know, slightly damp sand is perfect for sculpting. Make a rough mound of sand and pat it firmly into a basic shape; the patting action presses air out of the sand, making it stronger. Can you transform the mound into a

mermaid, a turtle, a fish or something else? Use a shell, a stick or even a spoon to add the finer details; a straw might come in handy for blowing sand out of awkward nooks and crannies. Add other details using shells, sticks, pebbles, seaweed or feathers.

beach picture frame

To make a special driftwood picture frame decorated with beach treasures, either tie everything in place with string and elastic bands at the beach, or stick it together with hot glue at home to make a lasting keepsake.

● Look through the magic frame at the beach to help you to choose strong views and images to photograph or paint.

● Place the frame on the sand and make a picture using collected beach materials; perhaps a fish made from shells (see page 52) or a driftwood dragon made from razor shell spines hiding among the seaweed trees. Try making special pictures on each beach you visit, photographing them as a reminder.

● Use the frame around a favourite beach photograph at home. Or you could make a permanent collage of beach treasures on a cardboard base to go inside your frame.

Safety tip Hot glue guns should only be used under close supervision by an adult.

mosaics and patterns

Many beaches are littered with loose treasures, such as shells, stones and pebbles of every shape, size and colour. Or beside a river you may find leaves, petals and seeds. Can you use nature's treasures to create wonderful patterns, mosaics and designs? There are more ideas to inspire you overleaf.

shadow pictures

Big open beaches are great places for shadow play on sunny days, particularly towards evening. Have a camera at the ready as the shadows won't last for long.

Water shadows Stand at the water's edge to make strange, distorted water shadows; the movement of the waves seems to bring the shadows to life.

Stick shadow monsters Push some sticks into the sand; can you transform them into shadow monsters using a few leaves or bits of seaweed?

Shadow sculptures When the sun is low in the sky, look for shells, stones, sticks or dry seaweed to design sculptures to cast long shadow patterns across the sand.

Shadow figures Can you use your body to make funny shadow monsters on the beach? Who can make the funniest monster?

39

beach textures

Look closely to see how many different natural patterns and textures you can spot at the beach, taking photographs of each one. Look out for sand ripples, eroded rocks, waves, pebbles, shells, reflections, water over sand and patterns in the sky.

How many different patterns, textures, colours and shapes can you spot? Can you put your pictures together into a collage? Make a competition for your friends; can they guess what all the patterns are? Send your best pictures to feature on the Going Wild website: www.goingwild.net.

trick photos

Play tricks on your friends with funny photos that fool the eye, making the big look small and the small look big!

Trick photos work best on a bright sunny day. How about a cloud ice cream, picking up a boat or stamping on a house? And is that a pizza or an island that Dan is eating? Or try photographing something that looks a bit strange, like this distorted underwater swimmer.

Trick photo challenge We would love to feature trick photos on the Going Wild Website; send your masterpieces to www.goingwild.net.

5

beach imagination

castles and forts

Everyone likes to build sand castles, but how many other sorts of castles can you build on sea, river and lake beaches?

Have a go at making rock turrets, pebble fortresses, river gravel castles, wet sand dribble towers and mud and stick forts. Or try building a castle somewhere more unusual, where marauding warriors would find it hard to ransack – perhaps on a rocky island or on a floating raft in the middle of a rock pool?

42

imaginary worlds

Mimi found a long conical shell, but she believed it was really a unicorn's horn. How about inventing a crazy magical scavenger hunt to get your imagination soaring? If you look carefully, perhaps you will find the things on the checklist below:

Miniature worlds Can you use your scavenged collections to create tiny houses and other details for imaginary worlds?

Scavenger hunt checklist

- ☐ A mermaid's beauty kit.
- ☐ A table laid for Neptune's banquet or a packed lunch for a sea nymph.
- ☐ The claws and fangs of a sea monster.
- ☐ A shell to magic you back to the sea from wherever you are!
- ☐ A beach hut or a parasol for a fairy's beach holiday.
- ☐ The lost jewel from Neptune's crown.
- ☐ Seaweed armour and shell and driftwood weapons for an elfin knight.
- ☐ A ball gown for a sea nymph.

43 storyboards

● They say a picture is worth a thousand words. A storyboard uses pictures instead of words to tell a story; this beach storyboard shows a surfer waiting in front of a fire for just the right wave. When the perfect wave comes along he has the ride of his life, not realizing that an enormous hungry shark lurks beneath the surface of the sea. At the end of the story there is a happy smiling shark with a very full tummy!

● Use pebbles and other natural materials to make a beach storyboard. Either make up your own story or tell a familiar one; Can your friends guess what your story is?

sand mermaids

Make yourself into a mermaid and then let the sea slowly transform you back into human form!

Sit down a little way from the sea line on an incoming tide and make a sandy mermaid tail over your legs. Race against the tide to make the best tail you possibly can, complete with fins and scales, before the incoming waves wash it all away. It's best to play this game on a warm day when the waves are small!

making magic boats

Just perfect for imaginary adventures in which you sail across the ocean to faraway lands with your friends; but watch out for attacking pirates!

Can you make the biggest sand boat you possibly can? Perhaps it's a canoe, a rowing boat, a racing boat with an outboard motor, or even a pirate ship. Don't forget to add a sail or an

outboard motor with a tiller, seats, and flags, and perhaps some shell decorations.

If you build your boat near the incoming sea, you can race against the tide to get it finished. Dig a deep channel all the way around the boat so that the incoming tide capsizes your boat into the waves or you have to surrender to the pirates!

46

toy explorers

Pack up some toy people or animals and take them off for an exciting beach expedition.

These little characters are exploring a river beach; imagine their surprise at finding a shark lying in wait for them after they had scrambled up a steep rocky peak! Perhaps your toys would like to set sail across a pool in a little boat, defend a sand castle against enemy hordes or discover the wonderful underwater world of a colourful rock pool?

beach kitchen and café

On the beach café menu today is a very special pebble burger with salty sea-washed bark cheese and crispy fried driftwood chips. And how about a refreshing pine needle smoothie with a sweet, freshly baked coral bun for dessert? What will you be serving up?

PROJECT

48 seaside stick puppets

Collect some sticks, seaweed and shells; can you tie them together with string to make crazy stick puppets? For longer lasting and more effective puppets, take your treasures home and use a hot glue gun to attach them to the sticks.

Safety tips Hot glue guns should only be used under close supervision by an adult.

headdresses and hats

How about making a slightly sinister Neptune's crown or a beautiful tiara for a mermaid? Make dramatic hats at the beach, or collect materials from different beaches and make a wonderful headdress at home as a reminder.

Cut a strip of corrugated cardboard about 10cm/4in wide and long enough to go around your head. Poke feathers down into the holes in the cardboard. Decorate the cardboard with shells, dried seaweed and other beach materials, sticking them on with double sided tape, or if you are doing this at home, you could use hot glue.

A few tips Create a central feature, perhaps with a large scallop shell. And perhaps some seaweed hanging down to look like a wig!

50

funny body characters

If you want to play a trick on someone who's having a quiet snooze, try giving them a funny face or turning bits of their body into crazy characters.

● With a little bit of imagination, a few pebbles, some seaweed and other beach bits and pieces, you can transform an unsuspecting sunbather's tummy button into a yawning little character with a wacky hair-do.

● Try photographing them before they wake up so you can play a joke on them later. Or make a stop-frame animation where you take lots of photos, changing one small detail each time. Just like poor big-eared Louisa here, who can't decide whether to smile or cry! Or use pebbles to transform someone's hand into a creature, like this evil-eyed monster!

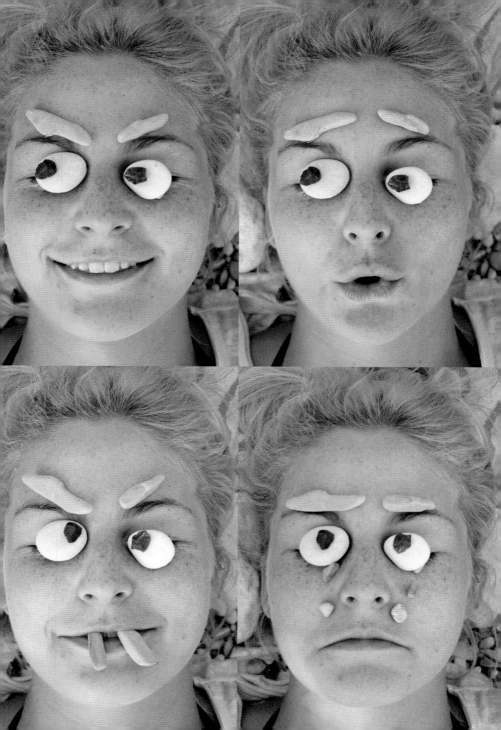

marram grass dolls

Marram grass stabilizes sand dunes. It is tough and flexible enough to be plaited and woven into little characters like this doll.

● Carefully cut a bundle of marram grass and tie a knot at one end; this will be the head.

● Split the grass stems into three bundles and plait them part of the way down to make a body. Now split the remainder into six bundles and make two plaits that will become the legs. Knot the ends to make feet.

● Take another, thinner, bundle of grasses; knot at one end then plait them together almost to the other end. Thread this plait through one of the loops in the upper body to make arms. Tie the loose ends in a knot.

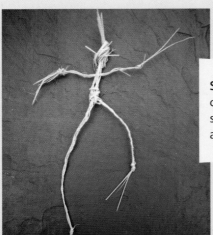

Safety tip Grasses can cause little cuts; avoid scraping grass edges along your fingers.

shadow transformers

Bring your shadow out to play on a sunny day!

● If you hold very still, perhaps your friends can transform your shadow into a monster or an imaginary creature. Make sure someone has a camera at the ready to capture each shadow's changing personalities.

● King Neptune here has a feather crown, a sand sword and shield. He has been joined by a lion who has a seaweed mane. In the evening, when the sun is lower in the sky, the lion transforms into a long-legged alien!

Shadow movie You could take lots of photos, changing the image a little each time, to create a stop-frame animation.

97

53

funny feet

Anyone walking past these giant funny feet just has to stop and try them on for size! This is a great way to get more people playing creative games at the beach.

Have a go at making all sorts of big feet, perhaps a pair of clumpy boots, some huge animal feet with long claws or giant's feet with horny toe nails. Make funny feet during a beach visit and see who comes along to try them on!

6

beach at night

54

night adventures

For a real adventure, head off to the beach after dark. Pack your bag with night lights, matches, a torch, plastic bottles, glow sticks and some binoculars.

When to go For the best and safest beach night adventures, go out on a clear, calm night when the tide is going out, preferably when the moon is full or the stars are bright.

Night walks Even at a beach you already know you will be surprised by how different it seems in the dark. Try not to use a torch; let your eyes adjust. Look out for the eerie glow of phosphorescence in the sea, and at river or lake beaches look for bats swooping low over the water to feed.

Moonshadow dancing In the light of a big full moon, use the beach as an enormous dance floor and make crazy moon shadows; best when you have the beach all to yourselves!

Stargazing Look up at the stars through binoculars.

Lie down on the beach with everyone's heads arranged like the spokes of a wheel. how many stars can you see?

Safety tips

- Beach night-time activities work best in dry, calm weather.
- Check the tide timetable; only go to the beach after dark when the tide is going out.
- Keep a close eye on the tide; the movement of the sea will be less obvious at night.
- Never leave candles, jars or any other belongings on the beach.
- Keep close together in a group. It's easier to keep an eye on everyone if each person wears a fluorescent armband or a glow stick bracelet.

Fire storytelling Sit around a fire to share scary stories; perhaps the wind is roaring and the waves are pounding as a bedraggled monster emerges from the sea…

Night swimming This is a wonderful activity at safe-swimming beaches without currents or waves. Always swim very close to the beach, with adults nearby.

flaming boats

This is a great adventure for a still night at low tide on a large rock pool, or at the edge of a river or lake.

● Cut a waxed juice or milk carton in half lengthways to make it look like a boat. Cover in tin foil (or use a foil container) and attach a long string to the front. Add a little sail if you wish.

● Make a 'power pack' by soaking a ball of cotton wool in methylated spirits. Place into the bottom and light just before you launch.

● Alternatively, place a night light on a little boat or raft. Cut the top part off a plastic bottle. Place it over the night light to make a little chimney, protecting the flame from the breeze. See page 101 top.

Safety tips

● Always keep the boats tethered so they don't drift off out of reach.
● Know when the tide is coming in.
● This activity must be supervised by adults.

56 glowing holes

These glowing holes look completely magical, but work best on a still, dry night.

● Push the top end of a plastic bottle down into slightly damp sand or gravel. Build up the sides a little around the bottle before removing it to leave a smooth-sided hole.

● Repeat to make a series of holes, perhaps in a line, a pattern or to spell out a word. Place a night light in each hole, and ask an adult to help you light them.

floating lanterns

Floating lanterns bring some magic to a night picnic. They work best in rock pools or in shallow, calm waters. If using them in open water, tether them so they won't drift away.

● You will need a clear plastic drinks bottle; there may be one among the picnic rubbish. Cut the bottle in half and discard the top. Put a little sand or a few pebbles in the bottom half; this will stop the lanterns from tipping over in the water.

● Place a night light on top of the sand or pebbles, and then light it and set the lantern afloat.

shining castles

Imagine a castle on a towering rock, glowing with a welcoming light, fit for a fairy princess!

● Choose a special spot for your castle; perhaps on a rock or in the middle of a pool. It's best to build the castle in the daytime and come back at night, but you will need to check that the tide won't wash it away.

● Take time to build the most impressive castle you have ever made, with tunnels, chambers and turrets. This fantastic castle perches on a steep-sided rock surrounded by water at the sea's edge.

● Put several nightlights into cut off plastic bottles; light them and then place them carefully inside the castle to create an atmospheric glow.

Perhaps you could wrap up warm and share a night picnic on the beach in the light of several glowing castles.

59

night games

Big open sandy beaches at low tide are perfect for night games of soccer, rugby or Frisbee; there won't be many people or dogs to get in the way! Take along some 'glow in the dark' balls, or try one of the following games with glow sticks:

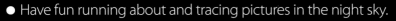

● Have fun running about and tracing pictures in the night sky.

● Tape some glow sticks to the outside of a Frisbee or perhaps a boomerang, being careful to balance the weight evenly.

● Put some water in a clear plastic drinks bottle (to add weight). Add a few glow sticks to make a rough and ready homemade glowing rugby ball (page 101).

Safety tip Make sure you know when the tide is coming in; this is not night water polo!

7

beach rubbish

rubbish rescue

Too many of the world's beaches are littered with plastic waste. Beach rubbish looks horrible and can be dangerous to wild animals and birds.

● Many local organizations often coordinate a Rubbish Rescue to tidy up the beach; you might be able to join in or you could organize your own beach clean-up. Take along a pair of gloves and a bin liner; you may even find something unusual and useful.

● Always remember to take all your rubbish home with you when you leave a beach. Perhaps you could make a picture like this to encourage more people not to litter.

rubbish sculptures

Look at rubbish in a new way by transforming it into wonderful sculptures.

The discovery of a life-sized rubbish horse with a pink flip-flop tongue and a thick coat of knotted ropes guarding the beach inspired us to make this crazy lion with its orange rope mane and rubber glove feet. What crazy rubbish creatures can you make?

Safety tips Only do these activities with adult help and check that the rubbish is clean and safe. Never collect plastic containers that have been used for storing toxic materials. Make this an opportunity to help clean up the beach too.

62

fun with picnic rubbish

Instead of bundling the picnic rubbish into a bag, try using it for all sorts of fun beach activities. Here are a few ideas:

Creative picnic rubbish
- Sand painting (see pages 64-65).
- Plastic bag flags and crisp packet streamers (see page 117).
- Bottle and carton skittles (see pages 40-41).
- Rubbish sand castle (see page 120).
- Bottle bucket, rock pool viewer and net (see pages 26-27).
- Plastic bag kites and wind socks (see pages 122-123).
- Make boats (see pages 118-119) and boat racing (see page 13).
- Rubbish pictures (page 114).
- Night activities (see pages 105-107 and 110-111).
- Don't forget to take all your rubbish home with you when you leave the beach.

streamers and flags

Have fun creating these shiny streamers to swirl around in the wind and little flags to decorate sandcastles and boats.

To make a streamer Cut open a crisp packet and lay it out flat. Cut round and round in a spiral until you have a long streamer. Attach the streamer to the stick as above, or use an elastic band. Run around with the streamers, place them on a sand boat (see page 88) or use them as decorations.

To make a flag Cut out a flag shape from a plastic bag or a crisp packet. Make a few small cuts along the fattest end of the flag and then weave a stick in and out (like running stitch) to fix as illustrated (left). These flags are perfect for castles (see page 108), to decorate a boat racing competition (see page 13), or to mark out a treasure trail (see page 42).

rubbish boats

Look through the picnic rubbish or wander along the tideline to look for clean rubbish to transform into little boats; plastic drinks bottles or waxed juice cartons are ideal.

Tie things together using string or connect them by piercing holes and pushing sticks through. Old corks or polystyrene add buoyancy and a plastic bag or a leaf makes a good sail. How about adding a passenger, perhaps made from a stick, a yoghurt pot or some seaweed?

Rubbish raft challenge

● Who can use bits of rubbish to make a raft that is sturdy enough to carry something heavy, perhaps a can of beans, your dad's shoes or mum's book? You will need a length of string to pull the raft along, unless you don't mind losing your selected items!

● Can your raft carry its cargo safely across the water, and keep it dry?

● Adding a keel will make these boats and rafts more stable. Make sure to take your boats home with you so you are helping to tidy the beach.

Safety tips Only float rubbish boats in shallow water.

65 rubbish sand castles

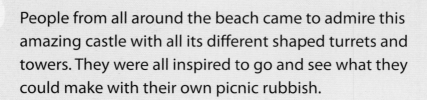

People from all around the beach came to admire this amazing castle with all its different shaped turrets and towers. They were all inspired to go and see what they could make with their own picnic rubbish.

● Collect lots of different-shaped containers, perhaps yoghurt pots, fruit and salad tubs, plastic lunch boxes or plastic bottles cut in half. Rinse them out if need be.

● Make a huge sandcastle and then decorate it by filling the different containers with slightly damp sand and tipping them out to make as many towers as you can. The more varied the shapes the more interesting your sand castle will be!

water bombs

Is your sister being boring just lying there sun bathing? A water fight will soon put a stop to that! Just fill some plastic bags and throw them at each other, great for a hot day.

Safety tips Remove all plastic bags from the beach after your water fight. Don't throw bags of water at people if they don't want to play.

67 kites

Big open beaches are perfect for kite flying. This little kite can be made from a plastic bag and some kebab skewers or drinking straws. You will also need some masking tape.

● Fix two skewers or two straws together in a cross. Cut a little off one length to make one axis longer than the other.

● Use a small amount of tape to attach the cross to an opened plastic bag. Cut the plastic bag into a diamond shape around the cross as shown.

● Poke a hole towards the bottom of the long axis of the kite, and another behind the cross. Make a loop of string through the holes. Attach a longer piece of string on to the loop and then go fly your kite!

wind socks

Feel the wind blow as you run along the beach with this fishy windsock.

● Cut off the bottom and top of a plastic bottle or yoghurt pot to make a cylinder about 15cm/6in long. Pierce a hole in each side of one end of the cylinder. Thread string through the holes to make a handle.

● Cut open a plastic bag to make a flat sheet. Fold in half lengthways and cut out a fish shape. Tape the long edges together so the wind will be able to blow through the mouth and out of the tail. Use staples or tape to attach the open mouth of the wind sock around the cylinder (see page 116).

● Decorate with bits of colourful plastic bag and long streamers.

Let the wind fill up your wind sock and bring it to life.

beach safety

Have fun at the beach, but please follow these guidelines to help you stay safe.

Beach safety guidelines
- Check the weather forecast before going to the beach. But remember that weather can be changeable, so you may wish to pack clothes and equipment for sun, rain and wind.
- Be aware of tides that can move very fast. Before going to a tidal beach, check tide timetables (available on the Internet and in local shops) so you won't get cut off by the tide.
- Only swim in safe swimming areas, and be aware of hazards such as undertows, currents, big waves and submerged rocks. Never jump or dive into shallow water.
- Watch out for jelly fish or other creatures or objects on the beach that might hurt your feet; wearing jelly shoes or wet boots is recommended.
- Be aware of hazards such as cliff edges, soft unstable cliffs, caves, soft mud and sand, and slippery seaweed covered rocks.
- Always have a first-aid kit handy, and someone who knows how to use it.
- Only use nightlights and candles when an adult is around to help.

Leaving no trace
Many beaches are wonderful wildlife habitats; always look after the natural world.
- Respect all wildlife.
- Be considerate to other users of the beach.
- Take all rubbish home with you.
- Take responsibility for your own actions.
- Only collect loose and plant materials that are common and in abundance.

Fire safety guidelines
Always follow these guidelines when using fire:

- Never make fire unless you have permission to do so and adults are around to supervise.
- Make fire on sand or mineral soil, in a pit or (preferably) in a fire pan. Be aware that pebbles and rocks can explode if heated to a high temperature.
- Never light a fire in windy or excessively dry weather conditions.
- Never leave a fire unattended.
- Have a supply of water nearby to extinguish the fire or soothe burns.
- Use as little wood as you can and let the fire burn down to ash. Once it is cold, remove all traces of your fire.

index

thanks and acknowledgments

Many thanks to:

The families and friends who have supported us in so many ways.

All the young people who took part in Beach Book activities: Monty and Daisy S; Alexander and Mimi D; Libby and George W; Hamish, Isobel and Oliver M; Ayrton and Edward K; Ama and Mahalia J; Susannah P; Tilly and Betsy S; Lydia, Helena and Lucien S; Sophie T; Edward and Rebecca W; Sienna, Bay and Lucas C; Sophie E; Lily, Toby and Charlie R; Natasha H; Louie C; Izzy G; Felix N; Carolyn S; Lucas R; Sam V; Amelia B; Clifford, Frankie and Anya C; and all those who agreed to be photographed but whose names we didn't manage to record.

The mystery beach artists whose work we came across in our wanderings; your work has inspired us and some pieces are included in this book.

Laura and Michael Danks, Simon Smith, Carol and Mike Furness and Louisa Reynolds for joyful days playing at the beach.

And huge thanks to our husbands, Ben and Peter, and our children, Jake, Dan, Connie, Hannah and Edward, for all their support.

And finally, thanks to everyone at Frances Lincoln.